Alber

Create Dangerously

Albert Camus was born in Algeria in 1913. He spent the early years of his life in North Africa, where he became a journalist. During World War II, he was one of the leading writers of the French Resistance and editor of *Combat,* an underground newspaper he helped found. His fiction, including *The Stranger, The Plague, The Fall,* and *Exile and the Kingdom;* his philosophical essays, *The Myth of Sisyphus* and *The Rebel;* and his plays have assured his preeminent position in modern letters. In 1957, Camus was awarded the Nobel Prize in Literature. On January 4, 1960, he was killed in a car accident.

ALSO BY ALBERT CAMUS

Notebooks, 1942–1951
(*Carnets, janvier 1942–mars 1951*) 1965

Notebooks, 1935–1942
(*Carnets, mai 1935–février 1942*) 1963

Resistance, Rebellion, and Death
(*Actuelles—a selection*) 1961

The Possessed (*Les Possédés*) 1960

Caligula and Three Other Plays
(*Caligula, Le Malentendu, L'État de siège, Les Justes*) 1958

Exile and the Kingdom (*L'Exil et le Royaume*) 1958

The Fall (*La Chute*) 1957

The Myth of Sisyphus (*Le Mythe de Sisyphe*) 1955

The Rebel (*L'Homme Révolté*) 1954

The Plague (*La Peste*) 1948

The Stranger (*L'Étranger*) 1946

Create Dangerously

Create Dangerously

THE POWER AND RESPONSIBILITY OF THE ARTIST

Albert Camus

Translated from the French by Sandra Smith

VINTAGE INTERNATIONAL

Vintage Books

A Division of Penguin Random House LLC

New York

FIRST VINTAGE INTERNATIONAL EDITION, OCTOBER 2019

Create Dangerously was first presented as a speech given at Uppsala University in Sweden on December 14, 1957, under the title "The Artist in His Times."

The Cataloging-in-Publication Data is on file at the Library of Congress.

Vintage International Trade Paperback ISBN: 978-1-9848-9738-1
eBook ISBN: 978-1-9848-9739-8

Book design by Nicholas Alguire

www.vintagebooks.com

Printed in the United States of America
5th Printing

Create Dangerously

When praying, a wise man from the East always implored his deity to spare him from living in interesting times. Since we are not wise men, our deity has not spared us, for we do live in interesting times. In any case, our era refuses to allow us to ignore it. The writers of today already know this. If they speak out, they are immediately criticized and attacked. If they remain silent out of humility, no one will ever speak of anything but their silence, to raucously reproach them.

Amid this blaring din, writers can no longer hope to stand on the sidelines to pursue the thoughts and reflections they cherish. Up until now, it has been more or less possible to remain detached from history. Anyone who disagreed with events could often remain silent, or speak of other things. Today, everything has changed: silence itself has taken on formidable meaning. The moment that remaining detached was considered a choice, and punished or praised as such, artists, whether they liked it or not, became *involved.* And in this, the word *involved* seems to me much more accurate than simply *committed.* In fact, it is not merely a matter of the artist's voluntary commitment, but rather of obligatory military service. All artists today have embarked in the galley of the times. They must resign themselves to that fact, even if they feel their ship reeks of rotten fish, that there are really too many tyrannical overseers, and, what is more, that they are headed off course. We are adrift on the open seas. Artists, like everyone else, must take up their oars, without dying, if possible—that is to say, by continuing to live and create.

To tell the truth, this is not easy, and I can understand how artists might miss their former comfortable life. The change has been rather brutal. Of course, in the amphitheater of history, there have always been martyrs and lions. The martyrs were given strength by the idea of eternal praise, the lions by very bloody historical fodder. But up until now, artists always remained on the sidelines. They sang for no reason, for their own pleasure, or, in the best of cases, to encourage the martyr and attempt to distract the lion from its prey. Now, on the contrary, artists find themselves trapped inside the amphitheater. Their voices, naturally, no longer sound the same: they are far less confident.

It is easy to see what art is at risk of losing in such continual involvement: their former comfort, mainly, and that divine freedom that lives and breathes in Mozart's works. We can now better understand the tormented and tenacious atmosphere of our works of art, their furrowed brow and sudden debacles. And so, we tell ourselves we understand that this is why there are more journalists than writers, more amateur painters than Cézannes, and why children's literature and murder mysteries have taken the place of Tolstoy's *War and Peace* or Stendhal's *The Charterhouse of Parma*. Of course, we can always counter this state of affairs with humanistic lamentation, to become what Stepan Trofimovich desperately wanted to symbolize in Dostoyevsky's *The Possessed*: reproach personified. And just like that character, we might also experience bouts of civic despondency. But that despondency would change nothing about what is really happening. It would be far better, in my opinion, to participate in our times, since our age is clamoring for us to do so, and quite loudly, by calmly accepting that the era of cherished masters, artists with camellias in their lapels and armchair geniuses, is over. To create today means to create dangerously. Every publication is a deliberate act, and that act makes us vulnerable to the passions of a century that forgives nothing. And so, the question is not to know whether taking action is or is not damaging to art. The question, to everyone who cannot live without art and all it signifies, is simply to know—given the strict controls of countless ideologies (so many cults, such solitude!)—how the enigmatic freedom of creation remains possible.

In this respect, it is not enough to simply say that art is threatened by the powers of the State. In fact, in that case, the problem would be simple: the artist would either fight or capitulate. The problem is more complex, more a matter of life and death as well, the moment we understand that the battle is being fought within artists themselves. The hatred of art, which has so many wonderful examples in our society, only thrives so well today because it is kept alive by artists themselves. The artists who preceded us had doubts, but what they doubted was their own talent. Artists of today doubt whether their art, and therefore their very existence, is necessary. The Racine of 1957 would apologize for having written *Berenice* instead of fighting for the Edict of Nantes.

This reassessment of art by artists has many reasons, but we will consider only the most important ones. In the best-case scenario, it is explained by the impression contemporary artists might have that they are lying or speaking for no reason if they do not take into account history's misfortunes. What characterizes our times, in fact, is the tension between contemporary sensitivities and the rise of the impoverished masses. We know they exist, whereas before, we tended to ignore them. And if we are aware of them, it is not because the elites, artistic elites or others, have become better. No, let's be clear about that—it is because the masses have become stronger and won't allow us to forget them.

There are other reasons for this abdication of responsibility as well, some of which are less noble. But whatever the reasons might be, they contribute to the same goal: to discourage free creative activity by attacking its principal essence, which is the creative artist's self-confidence. As Emerson put it so magnificently: "Man's obedience to his own genius is the ultimate definition of faith." And another American writer from the nineteenth century added: "As long as a man remains faithful to himself, everything works to his advantage: government, society, even the sun, the moon and the stars." Such prodigious optimism seems dead today. Artists, in most cases, are ashamed of themselves and their privileges, if they have any. Most importantly, they must answer the question they ask of themselves: Is art a deceitful luxury?

I

The most important honest response possible is this: it does, in fact, sometimes happen that art is a deceitful luxury. As we well know, we can, anywhere and forever, admire the constellations from the rear deck of the galley while the slaves in the hold keep rowing, growing more and more exhausted; we can always hear the worldly conversations taking place in the seats of the amphitheater while the lion's teeth tear into his victim. And it is very difficult to object about something in art that has known such great success in the past. Except for this: things have changed somewhat, and, in particular, the number of slaves and martyrs throughout the world has increased tremendously. In the face of such misery, art—if it wishes to continue to be a luxury—must today accept that it is also deceitful.

What would art speak of, in fact? If it were to conform to what the majority of our society asks of it, art would be merely entertaining, without substance. If artists were to blindly reject society, and choose to isolate themselves in their dreams, they would express nothing but negativity. We would thus have only the works of entertainers or experts in the theory of form, which, in both cases, would result in art being cut off from the reality of life. For nearly a century now, we have been living in a society that is not even the society of money (money and gold can arouse human passions); rather, it is a society full of the abstract symbols of money. Consumer society can be defined as a society in which objects disappear and are replaced by symbols. When the ruling class no longer measures its wealth in acres of land or gold bars, but rather by how many digits ideally correspond to a certain number of financial transactions, then that society immediately links itself to a certain kind of trickery at the very heart of its experience and its world. A society based on symbols is, in its essence, an artificial society in which the physical truth of humankind becomes a hoax.

We would then not be at all surprised to learn that such a society had chosen a type of morality based on formal principles, which it then turns into its religion; and such a society would inscribe the words *freedom* and *equality* on both its prisons and its hallowed financial institutions. However, these words cannot be prostituted with impunity. The value that is most vilified today is most certainly the value of freedom. Thinking people—I've always thought that there are two kinds of intelligence, intelligent intelligence and stupid intelligence—hold as a doctrine that freedom is nothing more than an obstacle on the path to true progress. But such solemn stupidities could only be put forward because for one hundred years, consumer society made an exclusive and unilateral use of freedom, considering it a right rather than an obligation and not fearing to use the principle of freedom to justify actual oppression—and as often as possible. From that point onward, is it truly surprising that such a society wished art to be not an instrument of liberation, but rather an exercise of little importance, simple entertainment? And so, all those high-society people who felt heartbroken over money or had emotional transactions were satisfied, for decades, with novelists who wrote about their world and produced the most useless kind of art imaginable. Oscar Wilde, thinking about himself before he went to prison, spoke of this kind of art, saying that the greatest of all vices was superficiality.

The manufacturers of bourgeois European art before and after 1900 (and note that I am not calling them artists) thus accepted their irresponsibility, because taking responsibility assumed a ruthless rupture with their society (and those who did make the break were the Rimbauds, the Nietzsches, the Strindbergs, and we know the price they paid for it). It was from that era that the theory known as "art for art's sake" was born, which was nothing more than an excuse for such irresponsibility. Art for art's sake, which was merely a pleasant distraction for the solitary artist, was precisely the contrived art of an abstract, artificial society. Its logical conclusion was the art of the "salons" (drawing rooms), or the purely formulaic art that is nourished by affectations and abstractions, and that finally results in the destruction of all reality. In this way, a few works please a few people, while a large number of clumsy inventions corrupt a great many more. In the end, art created outside of society cuts itself off from its living roots. Little by little, artists, even the most celebrated ones, find themselves alone, or at least are no longer famous in their own countries except through the intermediary of the popular press or radio, which provide a simplified, convenient idea of them. The more art becomes specialized, in fact, the greater its need to become popularized. In this way, millions of people believe that they know some great artists of our times because they read in the newspapers that they raised canaries or only ever remained married to someone for six months. Today, the greatest fame consists of being admired or detested without having been read. Artists interested in becoming famous in our society should know that it is not they who will become famous, but another version of themselves with the same name, and that other version will eventually take over and perhaps, one day, kill the true artist within them.

How surprising, then, that almost everything of any value created in the commercial Europe of the nineteenth and twentieth centuries, in literature, for example, was constructed to stand against the society of its times! Until the advent of the French Revolution, it could be said that modern literature was, on the whole, a literature of consent. On the other hand, from the moment the middle classes rose up, as a result of the revolution, and became stable, a literature of revolt began to emerge. Official values were then rejected, in France, for example, either by those who held to the revolutionary principles, from the romantic writers to Rimbaud, or by those who maintained aristocratic values—and in this, Vigny and Balzac are good examples. In both cases, the working classes and the aristocracy, which are the basis of any civilization, stood against the deceitful society of their times.

But this rejection, which has been supported and unyielding for such a long time, has also become deceitful, and has led to another kind of sterility. The theme of the cursed, scorned poet born into a consumer society (Alfred de Vigny's *Chatterton* is the best example) has become a rigid prejudice that ends up assuming it is impossible to be a great artist unless you stand against the society of your times, whatever that society might be. Legitimate at first, when it affirmed that a true artist could not make concessions to money, the principle became false when people also drew the conclusion that artists could only assert themselves by being against everything in general. This is why many of our artists aspire to be scorned, have a bad conscience if they aren't, and wish, at the same time, to be both applauded and booed. Naturally, society, which is today weary or indifferent, only applauds or jeers by a quirk of fate. The intellectuals of our times are thus endlessly hardening their positions to bring glory upon themselves. But due to their rejection of everything, including the traditions of their own art, contemporary artists give themselves the illusion of creating their own rules, so they end up believing they are God. At the same time, they believe they can create their own reality. However, if distanced from their own society, they will only create formal or abstract works, works that might be poignant as experiences, but that lack the fecundity that is characteristic of true art, whose mission is to unite. To sum up, there are as many differences between contemporary subtleties and abstractions and the works of a Tolstoy or a Molière as between the expected profit on an invisible crop and the rich soil of the furrow itself.

II

Art can, in this way, be a deceitful luxury. So it is not surprising that some individuals and artists wished to backpedal and return to the truth. From that moment on, they rejected the idea that artists have the right to stand alone, and offered them, as a subject, not their personal dreams, but the reality that was lived and suffered by everyone. Convinced that art for art's sake, in both its themes and style, was incomprehensible to the masses, or expressed nothing of their truth, those people wished, on the contrary, that artists would give themselves the task of speaking of and for the greatest number. If artists could translate the suffering and happiness of everyone in the language of the people, then they would be understood by all. As a reward for their absolute loyalty to reality, artists would succeed in creating global communication between people.

This ideal of global communication is, in fact, the ideal of every great artist. Contrary to current prejudicial ideas, the people who do *not* have the right to stand alone are precisely the artists. Art cannot be a monologue. When even isolated and unknown artists appeal to posterity, they are doing nothing more than reaffirming the very meaning of their work. Because they consider that a dialogue with deaf or distracted contemporaries is impossible, they appeal for greater dialogues with generations to come.

But to speak to everyone about everyone, it is necessary to speak of what everyone knows and the reality that is common to us all. The sea, the rain, our needs and desires, the struggle against death—these are the things that unite us. We resemble each other through what we see together, the things we suffer through together. Dreams change according to the person, but the reality of the world is our common ground. The goal of realism is thus legitimate, for it is inextricably linked to the artistic experience.

So let us be realistic. Or rather, let us try to be, if that is at all possible. For it is not certain that realism has a meaning, not certain it is possible, even if it is desired. Let us first ask ourselves if pure realism is possible in art. If we are to believe the assertions of the nineteenth-century naturalists, realism is the exact reproduction of reality. In that way, realism would be to art what photography is to painting: naturalism reproduces while painting makes choices. But what exactly is it reproducing, and what is reality? After all, even the best photographs fail to be the best reproductions, and, moreover, fail to faithfully reproduce reality. What is more real in our universe than a person's life, for example, and how could we hope to better render a life than in a realistic film?

But under what conditions would such a film be possible? Under purely imaginary conditions. In fact, we would have to assume there was an ideal camera filming a person, day and night, endlessly capturing every slightest movement. The result would be a film that itself would last that person's entire lifetime, and could only be seen by spectators resigned to sacrificing their own lives to be exclusively interested in the details of someone else's existence. Even under those conditions, such an unimaginable film would not be realistic, for the simple reason that life is not only found where a person happens to be. Life is also found in the other lives that give shape to theirs—the lives of loved ones, most importantly, that would have to be filmed, and the lives of the people we do not know as well: the powerful and the poor, fellow citizens, policemen, professors, the invisible companions who work in the mines and on building sites, diplomats and dictators, religious reformers, artists who create the determining factors of our behavior, and finally, the humble representatives of all-powerful chance, or luck, which rules over the existence of even the most organized of people. And so, there is only one realistic film possible: the film that is endlessly shown to us by an invisible camera on the screen of the world. The only realistic artist would be God, if he exists. The other artists are, of necessity, unfaithful to reality.

Consequently, artists who reject bourgeois society and its formal art, artists who wish to speak of reality and only of reality, find themselves at a difficult impasse. They must be realists but cannot be. They wish their art to be subservient to reality, but it is impossible to describe reality without making a choice that causes reality to be subservient to the originality of art. The beautiful, tragic works of art of the early years of the Russian Revolution demonstrate this struggle to us. What Russia gave us at that time, with Blok and the great Pasternak, Mayakovsky and Yesenin, Eisenstein and the first novelists of concrete and steel, was a splendid laboratory of forms and themes, abundant creative uneasiness, a passion for research. Yet it was necessary to follow through and show how it was possible to be realistic when realism was impossible. Dictatorship, in this instance as everywhere, took drastic measures: it stated that realism was primarily a necessity, and therefore possible, but on the condition that it intended to be socialistic. What was the meaning of such a decree?

In fact, such a decree openly recognizes that it is impossible to reproduce reality without making a choice, and it rejects the theory of realism as it was formulated in the nineteenth century. And so, all that was needed was to find a principle of choice around which the world could be structured. And such a choice *was* found, though not in reality as we know it, but in the reality to come, that is to say, the future. In order to properly replicate what exists now, it is also necessary to depict what is to come. In other words, the true object of the movement in art known as "social realism" is precisely a reality that does not yet exist.

The contradiction is rather superb, since the very term "social realism" was, in the end, contradictory. How, in fact, is "social realism" possible when reality is not entirely socialistic? Reality is not socialistic, for example, in the past, nor completely in the present. The answer is simple: from the reality of today or yesterday, we will choose whatever lays the groundwork and serves the perfect city of the future. In this way, we will devote ourselves, on the one hand, to rejecting and condemning whatever is not socialistic in reality, while exalting what is, or will become so. Inevitably, we will end up with the kind of art that is mainly propaganda, with its good and evil people—pedagogical literature, in sum, that is just as cut off from complex, living reality as formal art. In the end, such art will be socialistic precisely to the extent that it is not realistic.

Such an aesthetic, which aimed to be realistic, would then become a new form of idealism, just as sterile, to a true artist, as bourgeois idealism. Reality is only ostensibly placed in a sovereign position so it can be more easily eliminated. Art then finds itself reduced to nothing. It serves, and by serving, becomes subjugated.

Only those who deliberately prevent themselves from describing reality will be called realists, and praised as such. The others will be censured, to the delight of the realists. Fame in a bourgeois society, which consists of either being misread or not read at all, will, in a totalitarian society, prevent others from being read. Here again, true art will become disfigured, or gagged, and global communication will be made impossible by the very people who most passionately desire it.

The simplest thing, in the face of such failure, would be to recognize that so-called social realism has little to do with great art, and that revolutionaries, in the very interest of the revolution, should seek a different aesthetic. On the contrary, however, it is well known that its defenders cry out that no art is possible outside the realm of social realism. Indeed, they shout it out. But it is my profound conviction that they do not believe this, and that they decided, in their hearts, that artistic values had to be subjugated to the values of revolutionary acts. If that had been clearly stated, the discussion would be easier. We could respect such a great renunciation by people who suffer too much from the contrast between the unhappiness of the masses and the privileges sometimes linked to the destiny of the artist, who reject the unbearable distance that separates those silenced by poverty and those whose vocation it is, on the contrary, to ever express themselves. Then we might be able to understand those people and try to communicate with them, try, for cxample, to tell them that the suppression of creative freedom is not, perhaps, the right way to overcome servitude, and until we can speak for all, it is stupid to take away the power to at least speak for some. Yes, social realism should admit its roots and that it is the twin brother of political realism. It sacrifices art for a purpose that is alien to art but that, on the scale of values, might appear a superior goal. In sum, it temporarily suppresses art so it may first support justice. When justice exists, in a future that is still unknown, art will be reborn. Where art is concerned, therefore, we apply that golden rule of contemporary intelligence that states that it is impossible to make an omelet without breaking a few eggs.

But such excellent common sense must not go too far. It seems to me that you do not need to break thousands of eggs to make one good omelet, and the quality of the chef is not determined by the number of broken eggshells. No: the artistic chefs of our time should be afraid that they might knock over more baskets of eggs than they wanted to, and that then, the omelet of civilization will never set, and that art, in the end, will never be brought back to life. Brutality is never temporary. It does not respect the boundaries set for it, and so it is natural that brutality will spread, first corrupting art, then life. Then, out of the misfortunes and bloodshed of humankind, we see born insignificant literature, frivolous newspapers, photographed portraits, and youth-club plays in which hatred replaces religion. Art then ends up in forced optimism, which is precisely the worst of indulgences, and the most pathetic of lies.

How can this surprise us? The suffering of

humankind is such an important subject that it seems no one could understand it, unless they were like Keats, so sensitive, it is said, that he could have reached out and touched pain itself. This is obvious when literature is controlled and used to bring official consolation for our pain. The lie of "art for art's sake" pretended to ignore evil and thus took responsibility for it. But the lie of the realists, even if they have the courage to recognize the current suffering of humankind, betrays it just as gravely, by using it to glorify the happiness of the future, which cannot be known by anyone, and thus validates all this trickery.

Two aesthetics have clashed with each other for a very long time: one that recommends a total rejection of real life and the other that claims to reject everything that is *not* real life. Neither, however, describes reality, and both result in the same lie and the suppression of art. Right-wing academia ignores the miserable conditions that left-wing academia puts to use. And in both cases, misery increases while art is obliterated.

III

Should we conclude that such a lie is the very essence of art? I would maintain, on the contrary, that the attitudes I have spoken of up until now are only lies to the extent that they have very little to do with art. So what is art? Nothing simple, that is certain. And it is even more difficult to understand that idea amid the cries of so many people who are fiercely determined to simplify everything. On the one hand, we desire that genius be grand and solitary; on the other hand, we call upon it to resemble everyone. Alas! Reality is more complex. And Balzac sums it up perfectly in one sentence: "Genius resembles everyone but no one resembles genius." It is the same for art, which is nothing without reality and without which reality has little meaning. How, in fact, could art do without reality and how could it be subservient to it? Artists choose their purpose as much as they are chosen by that purpose. In a certain way, art is a revolt against the world in that it encompasses what is fleeting and unfinished: art does not, therefore, take on anything more than the purpose of giving another shape to a reality that it is, nevertheless, constrained to conserve, because reality is the source of art's emotion. In this respect, we are all realists and no one is a realist. Art is neither total rejection nor total acceptance of what is. It is both rejection and acceptance, at one and the same time, and that is why it can be continually and perpetually torn apart. Artists always find themselves dealing with this ambiguity, incapable of rejecting what is real, yet still devoted to challenging the ever-unfinished aspects of reality. To paint a still life, a painter and an apple must confront and adjust to each other. And if their shapes are nothing without the light of the world, those shapes, in turn, add to that light. The real world, which gives life to bodies and statues through its splendor, also receives another source of light that mirrors the light from the sky. Great style thus lies midway between artists and their objects.

It is therefore not a matter of knowing whether art should flee from reality or subjugate itself to it, but only the precise extent to which a work of art should weigh itself down in reality, so that it does not disappear into the clouds or, on the contrary, drag itself around in leaden shoes. All artists must find the solution to this problem according to their sensitivities and abilities. The greater an artist's revolt against the reality of the world, the greater the weight of that reality needed to counterbalance it. But that weight can never overpower the unique requirements of the artist.

Just as in Greek tragedy, Melville, Tolstoy, or Molière, the greatest work of art will always be the one that balances reality and the rebellion that mankind places in opposition to that reality, each causing a mutual and endless resurgence within each other, a resurgence that is the very definition of joyful yet heartbreaking life. Every now and then, a new world emerges, a world that is different from our everyday world, yet the same, unique but universal, full of innocent insecurity, born for a brief moment thanks to the strength and dissatisfaction of the genius. It *is* something and yet it is *not* something—the world is nothing and the world is everything. Such is the dual, tireless cry of all true artists, the cry that keeps them standing, eyes wide open, and that, from time to time, awakens in everyone, deep within the heart of this sleepy world, the insistent yet fleeting image of a reality that we recognize without having ever experienced it.

In the same way, artists faced by their times can neither turn away from nor become lost in them. If they turn away, they are speaking in a void. But, on the other hand, to the extent to which they accept reality as an object, they affirm their own existence as a subject, and will not completely subjugate themselves to it. To put it another way, it is at the very moment when artists choose to share the fate of everyone that they affirm their own individuality. And they cannot escape this paradox. Artists take from history what they can see or suffer themselves, directly or indirectly, that is to say, current events (in the strictest sense of those words) as well as what is happening to people alive today, and not the relationship between current events and a future that is unknowable to the living artist. Judging contemporary people in the name of those who do not yet exist is the role of prophecy. True artists can only value the dreams proposed to them in relation to their effects on the living. A prophet, priest, or politician can judge absolutely, and moreover, as we well know, they do not refrain from doing so. But artists cannot. If they judged absolutely, they would classify the nuances of reality as either good or evil, with nothing in between, thus creating melodrama.

The goal of art, on the contrary, is not to establish rules or to reign; it is first and foremost to understand. Art does sometimes reign, but precisely because it has achieved understanding. But no magnificent work of art has ever been founded on hatred or contempt. That is why artists, as they reach the end of their personal journeys, give absolution instead of condemning. They are not judges, simply justifiers. Artists are the perpetual defenders of living creatures, precisely because those creatures are alive. They truly advocate to love whoever is close by right now, and not those far in the future, which is what debases contemporary humanism, turning it into a catechism of the courthouse. Quite the reverse: a great work of art ends up baffling all the judges. At the same time, through such great works, artists give homage to the finest example of humankind and bow down to the worst criminals. As Oscar Wilde wrote from prison: "There is not a single man among these unfortunate people locked up with me in this miserable place who does not have a symbolic relationship with the secret of life." Yes, and that secret of life coincides with the secret of art.

For 150 years, the writers of consumer society, with very few exceptions, believed they could live in blissful irresponsibility. They did live, in fact, and then died alone, just as they had lived. But we, the writers of the twentieth century, will no longer ever be alone. Quite the contrary: we must know that we cannot hide away from communal misery, and that our sole justification, if one exists, is to speak out, as best we can, for those who cannot. And we must do this for everyone who is suffering at this very moment, despite the past or future greatness of the states or political parties that are oppressing them: to artists, there are no privileged torturers. That is why beauty, even today, especially today, can serve no political party; it only serves, in the long or short term, the pain or freedom of humankind. The only committed artists are those who, without refusing to take up arms, at least refuse to join the regular army, that is, they refuse to become snipers. And so, the lesson artists learn from beauty, if it is honestly learned, is not the lesson of egotism but of solid brotherhood. When conceived in this way, beauty has never enslaved anyone. Quite the opposite. On every day, at every moment, for thousands of years, beauty has consoled millions of people in their servitude, and, sometimes, even freed some of them forever.

In the end, perhaps we are here touching upon the greatness of art, in the perpetual tension between beauty and pain, human love and the madness of creation, unbearable solitude and the exhausting crowd, rejection and consent. Art develops between two chasms: frivolity and propaganda. Along the high ridge where great artists keep moving forward, every step is dangerous, extremely risky. Yet it is within that risk, and only there, that true artistic freedom lies. A difficult kind of freedom that seems more like an ascetic discipline? What artist would deny that? What artist would dare claim to be equal to that endless task? Such freedom assumes a healthy mind and body, a style that would reveal a strength of the soul and patient defiance. Like all freedom, it is a never-ending risk, a grueling experience, and that is why today we flee from such risk, just as we flee from freedom, which demands so much of us, and instead, rush headlong into all kinds of enslavement, to at least obtain some comfort in our souls.

But if art is not a dangerous adventure, then what is it, and what is its justification? No, free artists cannot enjoy comfort any more than free people can. Free artists are those who, with great difficulty, create order themselves. The more chaos they must bring order to, the stricter their rules will be, and the more they will have affirmed their freedom. Gide said something that I have always agreed with, even though it might be misunderstood: "Art lives from constraint and dies from freedom." That is true, but we must not draw the conclusion that art should be controlled. Art only lives through the constraints it places upon itself: it dies from any others. On the other hand, if art does not control itself, it descends into madness and is enslaved by its own illusions. The most liberated form of art, and the most rebellious, will thus be the most enduring; it will glorify the greatest effort.

If a society and its artists do not accept this long, liberating task, if they yield to the comforts of entertainment or conformity, to the diversions of art for art's sake or the moralizing of realistic art, its artists will remain entrenched in nihilism and sterility. Saying this means that a rebirth in art today depends on our courage and our desire to see clearly.

Yes, that rebirth is in all our hands. It is up to us if the West is to inspire resisters to the new Alexander the Greats who must once more secure the Gordian knot of civilization that has been torn apart by the power of the sword. To accomplish this, we must all run every risk and work to create freedom. It is not a question of knowing whether, while seeking justice, we will manage to preserve freedom. It *is* a question of knowing that without freedom, we will accomplish nothing, but will lose, simultaneously, future justice and the beauty of the past. Freedom alone can save humankind from isolation, and isolation in its many forms encourages servitude. But art, because of the inherent freedom that is its very essence, as I have tried to explain, unites, wherever tyranny divides. So how could it be surprising that art is the chosen enemy of every kind of oppression? How could it be surprising that artists and intellectuals are the primary victims of modern tyrannies, whether they are right-wing or left-wing? Tyrants know that great works embody a force for emancipation that is only mysterious to those who do not worship art. Every great work of art makes humanity richer and more admirable, and that is its only secret. And even thousands of concentration camps and prison cells cannot obliterate this deeply moving testimony to dignity. That is why it is not true that we could, even temporarily, set culture aside in order to prepare a new form of culture. It is impossible to set aside the endless testimony of human misery and greatness, impossible to stop breathing. Culture does not exist without its heritage, and we cannot, and must not, reject our own, the culture of the West. Whatever the great works of art of the future might be, they will all contain the same secret, forged by courage and freedom, nourished by the daring of thousands of artists from every century and every nation. Yes, when modern tyrannies point out that artists, even when confined to their profession, are the public enemy, they are right. But they also pay homage, through the artist, to an image of humankind that nothing, up until now, has had the power to destroy.

My conclusion will be simple. It suffices to say, in the very midst of the sound and fury of our times: "rejoice." Rejoice, indeed, at having witnessed the death of a comfortable, deceitful Europe, and at facing cruel truths. Rejoice as people, because a lie that lasted for a long time has crumbled, and we can now clearly see what is threatening us. And rejoice as artists, awakened from our sleep and cured of our deafness, so we are forced to face misery, prisons, and bloodshed. If, in the presence of that spectacle, we can preserve the memory of those days and faces, and if, on the contrary, seeing the beauty of the world, we can always remember those who were humiliated, then Western art will gradually regain its strength and its majesty. Surely, throughout history, there are few examples of artists who faced such difficult problems. But it is precisely because even the simplest words and phrases are weighed in terms of freedom and bloodshed that the artist learns to use them with careful consideration. Danger leads to becoming exemplary, and every type of greatness, in the end, has its roots in taking risks.

The days of irresponsible artists are over. We will miss the brief moments of happiness they brought us. But at the same time, we will recognize that this ordeal has given us the possibility of being truthful, and we will accept that challenge. Freedom in art is worth very little when it has no meaning other than assuring that the artist has an easy life. For a value, or a virtue, to take root in any society, we must not lie about it, which means we must pay for it, at every possible moment. If freedom has become dangerous, then it is on the verge of no longer being prostituted. And I could not, for example, agree with people today who complain about the decline of wisdom. Apparently, they are right. But, in truth, wisdom has never declined as much as at those times when it was a pleasure without risks to a handful of humanists who had their heads buried in books. But today, when wisdom finally must face real dangers, there is a chance, on the contrary, for it to once again stand tall, once again be respected.

It is said that Nietzsche, after he parted from Lou Salomé, descended into irrevocable loneliness, simultaneously crushed and exalted at the idea of the immense work of art he would have to undertake with no help, and that at night, he would walk in the mountains that overlooked the Gulf of Genoa, lighting great fires of leaves and branches that he would watch burn and disappear. I have often thought about those fires and sometimes imagined certain people and certain works of art standing in front of them, to test them. Well, our age is one of those fires whose indefensible flames will probably reduce many great works of art to ashes! But the works that survive will remain strong and intact, and when describing them, we will be able, without hesitation, to revel in that supreme joy of the intelligence we call "admiration."

We may hope, of course, as I do, for smaller flames, a moment of respite, a pause that will allow us to dream again. But perhaps there is no peace for an artist other than the peace found in the heat of combat. "Every wall is a door," Emerson rightly said. Do not seek the door, or the way out anywhere but in the wall that surrounds us. On the contrary, let us seek respite wherever it exists, that is, in the very heart of the battle. For in my opinion, and this is where I will conclude, *that* is where respite can be found. It is said that great ideas come to the world on the wings of a dove. And so, perhaps, if we listen closely, amid the din of empires and nations, we might hear the faint sound of beating wings, the sweet stirrings of life and hope. Some will say that such hope is carried by a nation, others by a person. But I believe quite the reverse: hope is awakened, given life, sustained, by the millions of individuals whose deeds and actions, every day, break down borders and refute the worst moments in history, to allow the truth—which is always in danger—to shine brightly, even if only fleetingly, the truth, which every individual builds for us all, created out of suffering and joy.

ALSO BY

ALBERT CAMUS

THE MYTH OF SISYPHUS

Featured here in a stand-alone edition, *The Myth of Sisyphus* is a crucial exposition of existentialist thought. These essays begin with a meditation on suicide—the question of living or not living in a universe devoid of order or meaning. With lyric eloquence, Albert Camus brilliantly posits a way out of despair, reaffirming the value of personal existence and the possibility of life lived with dignity and authenticity.

Nonfiction

THE FIRST MAN

Jacques Cormery is a boy who lived a life much like Camus's own: a childhood marked by poverty, a father's death yet redeemed by the austere beauty of Algeria, and the boy's attachment to his nearly deaf-mute mother. Published thirty-five years after its discovery amid the wreckage of the car accident that killed Camus, *The First Man* is the consummation of this great novelist's life and work.

Fiction

RESISTANCE, REBELLION, AND DEATH

Essays

In the speech he gave upon accepting the Nobel Prize in Literature in 1957, Albert Camus said that a writer "cannot serve today those who make history; he must serve those who are subject to it." And in these twenty-three political essays, he demonstrates his commitment to history's victims, from the fallen *maquis* of the French Resistance to the casualties of the Cold War. *Resistance, Rebellion, and Death* displays Camus's rigorous moral intelligence, addressing issues that range from colonial warfare in Algeria to the social cancer of capital punishment. But this stirring book is, above all, a reflection on the problem of freedom and, as such, belongs in the same tradition as the works that gave Camus his reputation as the conscience of our century: *The Stranger*, *The Rebel*, and *The Myth of Sisyphus*.

Nonfiction

THE STRANGER

Since it was first published in English in 1946, Albert Camus's first novel, *The Stranger*, has had a profound impact on millions of readers. Through this story of an ordinary man who unwittingly gets drawn into a senseless murder on a sun-drenched Algerian beach, Camus explored what he termed "the nakedness of man faced with the absurd." Now, in an illuminating American translation, extraordinary for its exactitude and clarity, the original intent of *The Stranger* is made more immediate.

Fiction

THE FALL

The Fall is a novel of the conscience of modern man in the face of evil. Clamence, an expatriate Frenchman, indulges in a calculated confession. He recalls his past life as a respected Parisian lawyer and, privately, a libertine—yet one apparently immune to judgment. As his narrative unfolds, ambiguities amass; every triumph reveals a failure, every motive a hidden treachery. The irony of his recital anticipates his downfall—and implicates us all.

Fiction

THE REBEL

An Essay on Man in Revolt

For Albert Camus, the urge to revolt is one of the "essential dimensions" of human nature, manifested in man's timeless Promethean struggle against the conditions of his existence, as well as the popular uprisings against established orders throughout history. And yet, with an eye toward the French Revolution and its regicides and deicides, he shows how inevitably the course of revolution leads to tyranny. As old regimes throughout the world collapse, *The Rebel* resonates as an ardent, eloquent, and supremely rational voice of conscience for our tumultuous times.

Nonfiction